© Al-Amanah Publishing
Chimayatul A Arifin
2023
Sydney, Australia
Email:
alamanahservicespublishing@gmail.com

ISBN: 978-0-6459356-0-8

# Contents

Nobody was born a champion
My hijab
Grief/loss
Seaside
The Scar
Mindset matters
Motherhood
The Seeker of Knowledge
Gone Angry
Movement
Coffee
Trigger
Spring
Miscarriage
The Darkness
Friendship
Dear Parents
A legacy
A prayer for you

# Nobody was born a champion

Experiences, challenges,
Moments, overcoming a fear,
A breakdown,
Happiness, joy
Moments of tears,

The struggles of a human soul,
Nobody can ever put a price tag,
Each one of us go through
what has been bestowed,
Some days are great,
And some days are not,
You can guide your fate,
To where you want it to go,

The soul of a champion
Is one who does not let their past
Dictate their current self,
Taking the good
And making it last.

Champions are those that had many struggles,
Despite the odds,
They choose to do Good, Be the good, spread the good.

Because they are the champions.

# My Hijab

The cloth that sits upon my head,
Has carried through times spoken and unsaid,
It has been a journey facing challenges and barriers,
But Allah (God) has chosen the women to be the carriers,
The visible mark that wraps our heads and chest,
We wear it sincerely, intentionally marking us from the rest,
It does not stop me doing the things I love,
As long as I put the intention in the actions for Al-Mighty above,
It does not matter that they think we are oppressed,
My hijab is my choice, my dignity and my way of loving Allah, and Allah knows Best.

# Grief/loss

There are so many emotions going
through my head,
Even when my body was done ..
Lying here in my bed,
I feel numb,
I feel pain,
Random moments
when I cry in vain,
It feels like a wave washes over me,
I feel it too much.. almost
I no longer fight it
I finally see..
Because I truly know
that soul returned
Where it's supposed to be..

# Seaside

Her shoes are off near the summer concrete..
She steps on the sand as
her feet are swallowed,
Her eyes look up onto the horizon,
She praises her Lord,
In awe
The sun begans to set,
pink, red and yellow
shades of the sky and sun all marry together ,
she walks towards the water
a wave catches her feet,
How beautiful is this seaside O Lord
you did create...

# The scar

The old scar is still there..
Sometimes no one else can understand what you bear..
In one moment can one's life crumble,
In the hands of a despicable other..
It was not easy to overcome,
embarassed or thinking you be shunned,
but when you realised you weren't at fault,
the amount of relief that leaves your chest,
indescribable emotions
Oh dear heart be at rest

## Mindset Matters

Our brains created
perfectly by Our Lord..
The control centre of our
physical beings.
When you open the mind,
Your willingness grows..
to grow with ideas
to flourish for better
but to also re-learn
unlearn unwanted patterns,
When you ask your Lord to
open your mind,
ask him freely to also open
your heart,
want more but want
better..
mindset matters

# Motherhood

It started from way before you were born..
thinking, planning and worrying..
Oh the worrying...
From walking around with you in my belly,
feet sore and swollen,
and then you finally arrived,
I did not know I could feel this way,
heart bursting, my body feeling euphoric
You start to grow I feel time slipping, the moments are going in the blink of an eye,
ya Rabb
savour and trying to be in the moments
my child my child
you will always be my love

# The seeker of Knowledge

Oh seeker of knowledge
how wonderful is your mind..
to be willingly determined,
To the wonders of the unknown..
but of course beneficial knowledge is the
dream of the seeker,
to learn
to unlearn
to practice and to preach
O seeker of knowledge May your Lord be
pleased with you

# Gone angry

I feel it rising in my chest..
the flood of blood pumps hard
like a race tracks..
a word of regret,
a regret of action,
the moment is lost,
the moment,
gone angry..
as the blood runs slow
you know you made a mistake..
but your ego runs deep
ashamed and embarrassed
it takes guts to right your wrongs,
the anger is gone..
Gone is the anger , peace has
come.

## Movement

Cardio ,weights, an afternoon walk..
whatever your liking, it's movement
of the body..
The body was created by Our Lord
to move,
Hundreds of muscle, tissues and
joints ..
How magnificent is this body of
ours,
remebering that the Lord has
bestowed,
Our bodies are indeed an Amanah,
a trust a responsiblity,
treat it well
there will be this only one

# Coffee

That first sip runs deep..
it glides down warming your
pipe to the belly..
savouring those special beans,
Like silk passing through each
time with a sip,
oh dear coffee
thank the Lord for your
presence
im a littler nicer than that
moment before..
Oh coffee
dearest coffee
many thanks to you

# Trigger

What is this thing you call a
trigger..
is it sadness,
is it anger,
was it an event..
Found out what,
maybe you need that
external help,
listen to yourself,
pause for a moment,
take a breath,
breathe in and out
close your eyes
thats it.. that's it..
you can feel yourself calm
down

# Spring

The tree outback the white petals are
blooming..
the days are warming
with parted clouds and sunshine...
the breeze gentle blows on the petals
of the spring trees,
can you smell that,
isn't the day like a warm hug,
thanking the Lord
Spring has sprung

# Miscarriage

It was an exciting time for our little
family ..
planning with joy and happiness..
little did we know,
the unexpected came,
a first small drops,
she did bled,
days went by and it came out more,
Dear Lord
what is the doctor saying
no heartbeat?
She sobbed and her body did shook,
a sudden feeling of emptiness,
my heart is only at peace
knowing we possibly
meet again

# The darkness

The darkness
is it a place,
is it a time,
we try our best
because we don't like the
darkness,
it pulls us away from our
natural state,
it is only human to fall
sometimes,
pick yourself up becaue
even in the dark there is
lightness found

# Friendship

A love for a friend is a
different love..
you are not blood related
but the bound can be
thicker than those of blood.
loving that friend for the
sake of your Lord
the laughters,
the advice,
the memories that were
created..
how honoured when our
Lord blesses us with good
companions

# Dear parents

To my beloved parents
you left your home land
to found a better ground..
it must not have been easy to
teach us the ways,
when our religion was the
opposite of what society
expects,
as I grow older I finally
understand,
the blood, sweat and tears
the sacrifices made
Dear Lord have mercy on them
just like that mercy on me when I
was young

# A legacy

I dream for a beautiful legacy
not of property
and not of wealth
but of abundace of teachings,
of character and ways,
till my time ends and even after
the days..
a continuous charity in the
name I was given,
I dream of a beautiful one,
this beautiful legacy
May the Lord give us this and more

# A prayer for you

I pray for the ones in sadness
I pray for the ones in sickness,
I pray for the ones lost, the ones that want to be found,
the grieving and the ones in constant pain,
I pray the Lord lessens your burdens,
releasing you from unnecessary shackles,
I hope in the end you are free from it all,
let their hearts be at ease ya Rabb.

# About the author

Chimayatul A Arifin also known as Mya Arifin is an Indonesian Australian living in Sydney. She is a woman's personal trainer, Islamic educator and youth mentor. Her passions also include education , volunteering and mental health. Salams my heart is her first self published book.

www.ingramcontent.com/pod-product-compliance
Lightning Source LLC
Chambersburg PA
CBHW051540010526
44107CB00064B/2801